ON THE ROYAL ROAD

ON THE ROYAL ROAD

A decade of photographing the Royal Family

TIM GRAHAM

LITTLE, BROWN AND COMPANY
BOSTON – TORONTO

FOR MY PARENTS

Half-title page Princess Anne at the Independence Day celebrations in The Gambia, February 1984.

Previous pages Prince Charles windsurfing at Cowes, September 1980.

Opposite The Queen in Poona during her visit to India in 1983.

Library of Congress Catalog Number 84–80878

First American Edition

Printed in Italy

CONTENTS

ACKNOWLEDGMENTS

My friends and colleagues know that I forget everything and they gave up years ago telling me anything of consequence. All important information is given to my memory – my partner, my co-conspirator, my darling wife, Eileen. Apart from running my library of royal pictures and being the best agent in the country, she manages at the same time to prevent our baby daughter Lucy from filing her rusks in with my pictures. My thanks also to Ann Wilson for all her help with the book and for her infinite patience, to Simon Bell for his excellent design and understanding of pictures, and to Felicity Luard without whom this book would still not be finished.

For all the help I have been given over many years and on numerous royal tours, my great thanks to the Press Office at Buckingham Palace, in particular to Michael Shea, the Queen's Press Secretary, Victor Chapman, Press Secretary to the Prince and Princess of Wales, John Haslam, Assistant Press Secretary to the Queen, and to Ann Neal, Felicity Simpson, Sarah Brennan and Julie Simpson.

My grateful thanks for help with passes and information to Patricia Behr of the Department of the Environment, Maggie McGlone of the Foreign Office, Louise Gold of the Racing Information Bureau, Liz Richards of British Equestrian Promotions, Devina Cannon of the British Horse Society, Major Loyd and the Guards Polo Club, John Ellis of Cowdray Park Polo, the Cirencester Polo Club, Beth Barrington-Haynes for her assistance on international polo days, Liz Hearn of Ascot Races, Douglas Lowe of the Braemar Games and Jim Gilmore at the Badminton Horse Trials.

I am grateful to the Central Office of Information's regional press officers around the UK who have helped me on countless royal occasions and to the many royal tour press liaison personnel from Australia to Abu Dhabi, Canada to Kiribati, New Zealand to Nauru who have been of great assistance.

For their top quality printing and processing and their ability to keep calm when I am intent on having a crisis, my thanks to Optikos and Downtown Darkroom. To all at Sygma in Paris and New York, who syndicate my pictures overseas, my thanks for being the best in the business. And a very special thank you for Frédérique d'Anglejan of Sygma – the other woman in my life! – who with great Gallic charm, hard work and a magic wand, converts my rolls of exposed film into front covers and magazine spreads.

Every picture in this book bears witness to my faith in Kodak film and Nikon camera equipment. My cameras and lenses have been shaken, rattled and rolled in aged aircraft, on bone-shattering Land Rover rides, and even by the occasional crash on to a pavement. It is at times like these that I am particularly thankful for Mike Allen, brilliant camera mechanic, who with great enthusiasm and speed has carefully nursed my Nikon equipment back to health after inadvertent but inevitable abuse.

And finally – in the hope that they each might buy a copy of this book on their expenses! – special mention for those photographers and journalists that I am lucky to have shared the journeys with and to have as friends: Andy, Anwar, Ashley, Arthur, Garth, Gavers, Graham, Grania, Harry, James, Jayne, Jimmy, Kenny, Ron, Steve and Steve and Terry, who for many years have put up with my funny and not so funny little ways and who have helped make this job a whole lot of fun.

INTRODUCTION

Photographing the Royal Family may appear to outsiders a glamorous job but there are occasions when it seems anything but that way to me as I set off in the early hours of a cold, damp morning struggling to carry as much as twenty kilos of camera equipment and knowing that there is likely to be a long wait ahead – possibly with no worthwhile picture at the end of it. Even so, there is plenty of excitement and satisfaction in this job and I would not change it for the world. The variety and challenge of the work are a continuing thrill for me and the hours spent waiting on photographers' stands or jostling for a good position to cover an arrival at a routine royal event are more than compensated for by the jobs that go well and the marvellous travel involved. Many of the spectacular places I have visited and sights I have been privileged to see form lasting memories.

I have seen the Pyramids and the Taj Mahal, the Himalayas – a breathtaking sight as their snow-capped peaks turned fiery red at sunrise – the remarkable ruins of Pompei, and the mystery that is Petra – a hidden city carved out of sandstone cliffs. I have witnessed the splendour and excitement of the Raja Perahera in Sri Lanka – a carnival of exquisitely decorated elephants, jugglers and fire-eaters – and the cold magnificence of Red Square and the Kremlin. My job has taken me into dozens of royal and presidential palaces around the world, into the inner sanctum of the Vatican for the Queen's historic meeting with the Pope, and barefoot into the Golden Temple at Amritsar. I have been moved by a tour of Mother Teresa's mission in Calcutta and humbled by a visit to a leper colony in The Gambia and by the sight of severely malnourished, suffering children in Upper Volta.

Each tour, each assignment, is different. I have enjoyed the ultimate in hospitality during my stay in the Sultan of Oman's guest palace, sipped the obligatory Singapore Sling (or two!) at Raffles Hotel, and been pampered in some of the best hotels in the world. But it is not all five-star luxury. On many a trip I have slept in cramped cars or Land Rovers, and in Upper Volta the floor of a mission house was my bed for the night. I have gone from having my eardrums assaulted by the whinings and gruntings of a Hercules transport plane which carried us round New Zealand, and risking life and limb in creaky old planes packed to the limit with photographers and their tonnage of camera gear, to travelling extremely first class on the Queen's Flight on the Kenya-Bangladesh-India tour.

I have stood under showers that never ran water and shared baths with aquatic specimens that might baffle David Attenborough. Just for the fun of it, I have ridden elephants and camels, donned a grass skirt in Tuvalu and read a newspaper while floating in the Dead Sea. And all this travel has broadened my palate, too. I have eaten – more out of interest than desire – roast camel in Bahrain, crocodile steak in Papua New Guinea, wildebeest in Kenya and the gastronomic delight of roast bat at a feast in the South Pacific (not many requests for second helpings!).

Undoubtedly rewarding too is knowing that with interest in the Royal Family growing ever greater, if I take a good royal photograph it will get used by a number of magazines and books. There is little that gives photographers more satisfaction than to see their work featured on front covers and special spreads in the prestigious publications of the world.

Like any other family, some members of the Royal Family are easier to photograph than others. They are almost always on the move during their public appearances, which means that most pictures of them have to be taken literally 'on the hoof'. The Queen Mother is well known as a photographers' favourite. On her public engagements she never seems rushed, taking the time to acknowledge the crowd and look towards the photographers, often with that famous smile. Her thoughtfulness won me over from the first days of my career photographing royalty. I had gone to cover the Queen Mother's arrival at the Royal Opera House, Covent Garden, and keen for a good picture, I had arrived very early to get a prime position. As she stepped from her car and I went to take the picture, I found to my dismay that my flash did not fire. My not-very-well-stifled groan alerted the Queen Mother and she stopped to ask if I would like to take another shot. I was eighteen years old, just started in the job, and it is an incident I have never forgotten.

The Princess of Wales has proved equally photogenic, and there is always a crush to get the latest picture of her whenever she makes a public appearance. Her stunning looks almost guarantee a good picture, provided that you can get an unobstructed view at the right moment. And that's a tale in itself. Since the best way to get a good position when covering the more 'popular' engagements is to be in place very early, it might mean waiting for up to three or four hours, sometimes in the cold and wet. This is when the repartee between photographers on the spot really gets going and it has cheered many a dull hour. The longer the wait, the greater the teasing, the more corny the jokes and the more embellished the stories of past triumphs and failures!

Distances vary greatly when photographing the Royal Family. Sometimes I am just a few feet from them – and I must by now be a familiar and possibly amusing sight to them as I stand draped with cameras, brandishing in the air my exposure meter to check and double check the light readings. At other times I might be working from 150 to 200 feet away from them, particularly on the more ceremonial occasions. I work with four cameras – always Nikons as I've found them undoubtedly the best for my job. Fitted to each camera is an electronic motor drive – worth its weight in gold, for it enables me to shoot up to six frames a second when necessary and to rewind film at speed. When photographing the Royal Family, there is no second chance if the picture is missed. I have two of the cameras round my neck and one on each shoulder; they are fitted with 85 mm, 180 mm, 300 mm and 600 mm lenses. Depending on the circumstances, the range of lenses enables me to shoot the general scene as well as close-ups of the Royal Family. Also with me will be wide angle lenses and flash guns, and for certain jobs a small aluminium stepladder to help me see over the heads of a crowd – useful for covering walkabouts and times when there are likely to be a great number of photographers present.

However hard I try, there will always be the pictures I miss and one incident that I could kick myself for happened during Prince Charles's tour of India in 1980. We were a week into the tour and several of us were feeling rough through lack of sleep and the change in diet and climate. The tour programme told us that Prince Charles's day would be taken up by a visit to a Hindustani machine tool factory, which pictorially didn't sound very promising! We skipped the day's events and flew straight on to Madras, the next point on the tour. The picture that you won't find in this book, and that we all missed, was of Prince Charles at the factory being 'crowned' with a gold turban. It would have made the cover of dozens of magazines around the world.

Some of the pictures that did not get away are included in the following pages and among them are many of my personal favourites. They are chosen for their association with particular events, people and places, as well as because I simply happen to like them, and I hope that they will enable others to share the satisfaction and fun I have had photographing the Royal Family over the years.

THE OFFICIAL ROUND

Every year the diaries of members of the Royal Family are filled with hundreds of public engagements that take them round the country meeting people from all walks of life. These official duties range widely, from attending glittering banquets and premières to tours of factories, hospitals and schools, visits to the armed forces, attendances at charity events and of course going on the ever-popular royal walkabout.

From the schedule of engagements sent to me regularly from Buckingham Palace, I draw up my own list. It is impossible to cover everything so I pick out the occasions that I think are of most public interest and that sound photographically promising. You soon get to know which situations are likely to produce the best pictures. Careful planning is very important. There are passes to be obtained, equipment to be organized and checked – film, cameras, wet weather gear if likely to be needed – and photographic positions to be decided on. A visit to the location beforehand is often worthwhile in choosing the best camera position for the job.

It is not always possible to do your own preparation. I could not travel as far as Dartmouth for a preliminary look at the parade ground where Prince Andrew would be one of the cadets in the passing out ceremony, so I phoned to check details. With typical naval accuracy, I was told the distance from the photographers' stand to Prince Andrew's position in the parade – 150 feet. That's a vast photographic distance to get the close-up picture of the Prince that I wanted as part of my coverage of his passing out parade. In the event I was the only photographer to bring a long enough lens – 1200 mm.

Occasionally, no amount of careful planning will help and then you have to rely on luck. I waited along with about thirty fellow photographers for over three hours for Princess Diana to arrive at the Victoria Palace Theatre. Just at the moment she stepped from her car, one of the theatre staff walked in front of my camera and in that second I missed the picture. Thoroughly fed up, I went off with colleagues for a meal and, with spirits lifted by a few glasses of wine, I returned with only minutes to spare before the Princess was to reappear. This time things seemed to have become worse. A row of large Welsh guards now stood along the pavement between the theatre and the car. I found a perch on a window-sill behind the crowd and from there the Princess could be glimpsed momentarily as she passed down the guard of honour. Luck was with me. As she appeared in a gap between the broad backs of the guardsmen, she smiled. I had time for just two frames before the moment was gone and the picture here is one of them.

The Princess of Wales leaves the Victoria Palace Theatre, London, in March 1982 after a charity performance of 'The Little Foxes' starring Elizabeth Taylor.

President and Mrs Reagan visited the Queen at Windsor Castle in June 1982. They are seen here at the welcoming ceremony in the Quadrangle as the American national anthem is played.

Accompanied by the Duke of Edinburgh, the Sultan of Oman steps along the Victoria Embankment to inspect a guard of honour at the start of his state visit in March 1982.

The Queen and President Reagan riding in Windsor Great Park during his visit. The Queen's horse, Burmese, is the one she uses for the Trooping the Colour ceremony, while the President is mounted on another of her favourite horses, Centennial. The British and American press were gathered to watch them ride by. Well used to protocol in the presence of a member of the Royal Family, the British contingent worked in silence. The Americans, always expecting a quote, shouted questions at both the President and the Queen. Reagan lingered to talk while the Queen decided that it was best to ignore such effrontery and rode on ahead.

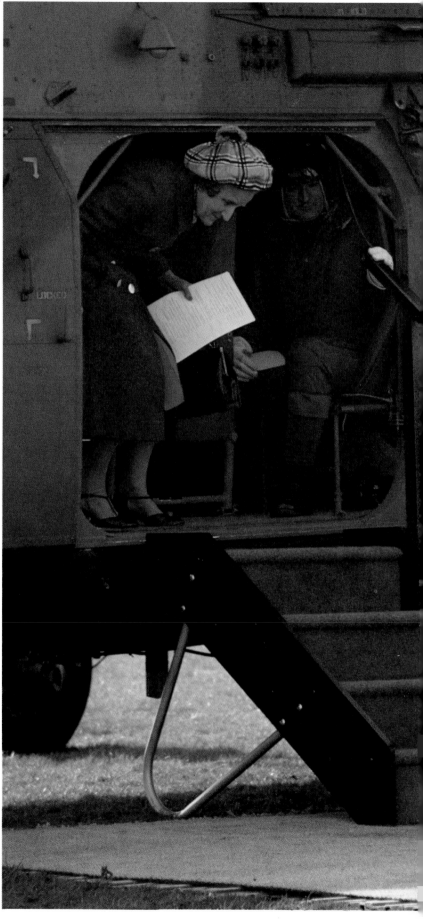

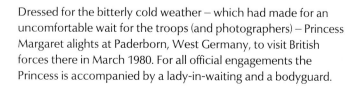

Dressed for the bitterly cold weather – which had made for an uncomfortable wait for the troops (and photographers) – Princess Margaret alights at Paderborn, West Germany, to visit British forces there in March 1980. For all official engagements the Princess is accompanied by a lady-in-waiting and a bodyguard.

Dressed for the occasion: Princess Alexandra photographed during her visit to Jersey in July 1983 (opposite); Princess Margaret at the re-opening of the Theatre Royal, Bath, November 1982; and the Queen Mother arriving at St Paul's Cathedral for the Falklands Memorial Service in July 1982.

Smiling through driving rain, the Princess of Wales returns to an awaiting helicopter after visiting Belgrave Lodge, a home for the elderly in Coventry, December 1982. It's the sense of crush and movement, with Princess Diana good-humoured despite the elements, that I particularly like here.

Opposite Prince Andrew in the passing out parade at Dartmouth Royal Naval College in April 1980; his parents, who had first met when Prince Philip was himself a Dartmouth cadet, were both present, and the Queen took the salute from her son and his colleagues.

Princess Anne arriving for the Garter Ceremony at Windsor Castle in 1974 accompanied by the Duchess of Beaufort *(left)*; and *(above)* at a garden fête in the Wiltshire village of her parents-in-law during the summer of 1975, two years after her marriage to Captain Mark Phillips.

Left Prince Charles was greeted with affectionate enthusiasm by a mentally handicapped boy during a visit to Merseyside in December 1982. This was one of those spontaneous moments that can happen on any assignment and are easily missed unless the camera is already to your eye.

Royal walkabouts always involve being on the watch for the stops to chat with the crowd: *(right)* Princess Diana on a visit to the Hearsay Centre run by Youth Aid in Catford, London, 1982; *(right below)* Prince Charles, in the uniform of Colonel-in-Chief of the Cheshire Regiment, joking with a couple in Canterbury, where he received the Freedom of the City in 1978.

Opposite An unremitting day of rain in Carmarthen failed to dampen Princess Diana's spirits on her first tour in October 1981, when Prince Charles introduced his new bride to Wales. Ignoring the shelter of umbrellas carried by her lady-in-waiting and bodyguard, she got drenched along with the enthusiastic crowd – and my Nikons. At the end of the day I had even used my shirt-tails in the effort to find something dry to wipe the camera lens.

The ever-photogenic Queen Mother was here on a visit to the Irish Guards stationed in Munster, West Germany, March 1984. It was St Patrick's Day and everyone sported shamrocks given by the Queen Mother.

POMP AND CIRCUMSTANCE

No matter how many times I watch the pomp and pageantry in Britain, I am never bored by it. To have a front row seat on such occasions is one of the perks of my job and though the ceremonies may follow the same, well-ordered pattern each time, they always offer a different photographic opportunity and challenge. Space limitations determine how many photographers can be present at a royal event and for big occasions there are not enough places to go round. The State Opening of Parliament is one event that I have so far not been able to cover and would dearly like to photograph.

With all these stately and much attended royal ceremonies, the photographers' stand is likely to be some distance from the action and it is usually only a very long lens – often my 600 mm – that will be useful. The Garter Ceremony, for example, is photographed from the battlements of Windsor Castle, a position I have used for many years and which gave me the charming informal picture of the Queen and Prince Philip battling cheerfully with blustery weather.

Trooping the Colour has the advantage of giving a full dress rehearsal the week before and since I cannot be in two places at once on the day, I usually photograph the rehearsal at Horse Guards Parade and take the photographers' position on the Victoria Memorial at the top of the Mall on the actual day of the ceremony. From there I can cover the outward and return processions, the Queen taking the salute by the gates of Buckingham Palace and the Royal Family standing on the balcony to watch the traditional flypast.

Members of the Royal Family travel in open carriages, weather permitting, to watch the ceremony at Horse Guards Parade. To get a good close-up in the carriage is at least a 600 mm shot, and a fast-moving carriage can make it quite tricky. You need double this focal length – 1200 mm – for a shot of the Royal Family on the balcony; the lens and camera have their own tripod to give stability and, hopefully, a sharp picture. Ideally, a 2000 mm lens is needed but the cost – around £5000 – for a lens that would probably be used only once a year makes it hopelessly uneconomic.

The Remembrance Day Service at the Cenotaph, November 1981; behind the Queen stand, from the left, the Duke of Kent, the Duke of Edinburgh, Prince Charles and Prince Michael of Kent. The solemn service is never easy to photograph but on this occasion the greyness of the November day was relieved by a shaft of sunlight.

The Garter Procession is held at Windsor Castle each June, when the knights of the Order of the Garter, the most senior order of knighthood, process with their attendants to St George's Chapel. Other than royalty, the members are limited to twenty-five knights, appointed independently by the Queen, and their distinguishing dark blue garter – worn on the left leg – carries the motto 'Honi soit qui mal y pense'. Prince Charles walks beside his grandmother in the Procession (*opposite*, in 1978, and, *above left*, in 1982), with the Queen accompanied by Prince Philip taking the final place of honour (*above right*, at the 1980 ceremony).

On such formal occasions it is often the personal glimpses, such as the obvious affection between the Queen Mother and Prince Charles or the shared amusement of the Queen and Prince Philip as they struggle with the windy weather, that make the picture.

Trooping the Colour, the ceremonial review of troops of the Household Division, is held each June at Horse Guards Parade to celebrate the Queen's official birthday. The Queen, wearing the uniform of Colonel-in-Chief of the Grenadier Guards at the 1983 ceremony, is escorted along the Mall back to Buckingham Palace (*right*), where she takes the royal salute (*above*).

Opposite Prince Charles at the Trooping the Colour
ceremony in 1980, as Colonel-in-Chief of the Welsh Guards,
one of the five regiments of Foot Guards belonging to the
Household Division.

The Queen Mother and the Princess of Wales drive back
from Horse Guards Parade after the 1983 ceremony; their
carriage proceeds along the Mall to Buckingham Palace
ahead of the Queen and her escort.

The Queen at Westminster Abbey in May 1982 for the Order of
the Bath ceremony; new members of this ancient order of
knighthood are installed in Henry VII's Chapel, where the banners
of the knights hang above the stalls. At one time knights would
take a ceremonial bath as a symbol of the purity of their vows,
and hence the name of the Order.

Holding the traditional nosegay of sweet-smelling flowers –
originally intended to ward off the smells of the unwashed masses
– Prince Philip attends the Maundy Service held in 1980 at
Worcester Cathedral. By ancient custom the Queen gives
Maundy money – now specially minted silver coins – to the poor
on this day.

Opposite ·The Queen at the Cenotaph in Whitehall during the
1981 Remembrance Day Service, her Flanders poppy forming the
only splash of colour in an otherwise sombre picture.

ON TOUR

Overseas tours, many of them to Commonwealth countries, are an important part of the Royal Family's timetable. They may last from a few days to seven or eight weeks, and the meticulous preparations for them may have gone on for months. I cannot claim anything like the Queen's own travelling record – she is the most widely travelled monarch in history – but over the last ten years I have visited over seventy countries, some of them several times. During one tour alone – Prince Charles and Princess Diana in Australia and New Zealand in 1983 – we had taken forty-nine flights by the time we reached home again.

A great advantage of all this is that I have been able to see many of the most beautiful and interesting sights in the world – the temples of India, the pyramids of Egypt, the wildlife of Africa, the islands of the South Pacific, a carnival of elephants in Sri Lanka, the splendours of the Vatican, to name but a few. Moreover, the host countries, unstinting in their welcome of the Royal Family, are seen at their best.

I like to arrive early whenever possible, which sometimes gives an amusing insight into the preparations. I was suitably impressed by the freshly painted façade and beautifully tended front garden of a tiny hotel that I was staying at in the South Pacific; the contrast with the sides and back was striking – the Queen was of course to see only the front! (In fairness, the hotel was shortly to be demolished to make way for a new Parliament building.) With great thoughtfulness, the same hotel had installed its first bar especially for the Queen's visit, or perhaps they had heard that the press like to gather round a gin and tonic or two at the end of the day. To repay their kindness we held an opening party at the bar, kitting ourselves out in grass skirts borrowed from the native dancers who had earlier performed for the Queen, and along with the British High Commissioner and his wife (similarly clad), we drank to the success of the bar, the success of the visit, the success of one another . . . we had plenty of time to kill before the next stop.

There are always surprises on royal tours and one of the most pleasant came during the Queen's visit to the Middle East. Arab hospitality extended to the forty or so members of the press corps, each of whom was presented with an individually wrapped, solid gold watch, distributed on behalf of our Arab host by a man from the Foreign Office who delved into a Harrod's carrier-bag to produce them!

More often things don't go our way. To follow Prince Charles's progress through the Sikh Golden Temple at Amritsar, the press were all requested to remove their shoes and socks. On a friend's advice I left mine in the car rather than at the Temple entrance and we had to put up with laughter from the others as we ran through the wet and unsavoury gutters barefoot. But we had the last laugh. The Prince left the Temple by another door and in the overwhelming crush of people and the scramble against time, some pressmen never found their shoes again. I gather too that the British ambassador in the Prince's entourage was last seen boarding the Queen's Flight with bare feet.

The Queen inspects the Royal Guard of Honour at Muscat Palace, Oman, during her tour of Eastern Arabia in February 1979.

The Queen in Arabia, February 1979

The Queen's three-week tour with the Duke of Edinburgh was her first visit to the male-dominated countries of the Middle East. *(Left)* Welcomed by the Amir of Bahrain on disembarking from the royal yacht *Britannia*; *(below)* watching horse and camel racing at Riyadh as guest of King Khalid of Saudi Arabia; *(bottom left)* the Duke of Edinburgh being entertained by the uncle of the Sultan of Oman. In Kuwait, the Queen visited the country's distinctively styled water reservoirs *(opposite)*, and attended a banquet given by Shaikh Jabir al Ahmed al Sabah *(bottom right)*.

Overleaf Discussing form at the racecourse with the Amir of Bahrain, who owned every horse running. Betting is against the Arab religion but the press corps had their own running book – which didn't go unnoticed by the Queen. She was later amused to learn that the naval photographer aboard *Britannia* – 'Snaps' as he is known to everyone including the Queen – had managed to relieve us of a considerable sum of money.

This was a difficult picture to take – I was shooting straight into the sun across the width of the racecourse, using a 500 mm lens – and I was pleased when it won for me 'Best Royal Photograph of 1979'.

Prince Charles in India and Nepal, November-December 1980

This long-awaited visit had been delayed until November 1980 because of political upheavals in India and despite some protest demonstrations, the Prince was greeted by increasingly enthusiastic crowds as the strenuous tour progressed. On the fifth day he visited the Taj Mahal, the Emperor Shah Jehan's memorial to his beloved Queen Mumtaz: 'a spectacularly beautiful idea to build something like this to someone you love' was the Prince's comment – to the delight of the press, which at this time was buzzing with rumours of an impending engagement to Lady Diana Spencer.

Prince Charles was happy to oblige photographers by posing before the marble monument in the position we had chosen for him beforehand. It was a compromise decision: it made him a very small figure against the Taj Mahal but the alternative – for us all to have been on the same narrow causeway as the Prince – would probably have resulted in one of us landing backwards in the water in the usual scramble for the best position. In retrospect, I think it would have been better if we had been on the causeway with the Prince, regardless of the risk – which never normally bothers us. That way, his image would have been much bolder against the Taj Mahal.

On any tour I cannot begin to relax until I have at least one picture that conjures up the flavour of the country. These pictures do not happen to order and sometimes it is possible to cover a whole tour without getting the definitive picture. Prince Charles is well aware of what makes a good picture and on a number of occasions has turned what would have been a fairly ordinary situation into something more visually interesting. *(Opposite)* The Prince is drinking coconut milk at Haripur, a village in the north-eastern state of Orissa, one of the poorest areas in India. *(Below)* He visits the Golden Temple at Amritsar, holy place of the Sikhs, where Prince Charles was presented with the long scarf accorded to the most honoured of guests.

Overleaf India at sunrise has a magical feel. It is a fascinating country and the drive through the dawn to get this picture of Prince Charles birdwatching by punt in the early morning light at Bharatpur, near Agra, was an added bonus on this tour. The large marshland, which dries up in the summer and floods during the monsoon season, was once the shooting preserve of the Maharajah of Bharatpur and, indicative of changing times, the visit of a previous Prince of Wales (later Edward VIII) in 1921 had been celebrated with a great duck shoot.

During his heavy programme, Prince Charles managed to fit in a game of polo, his favourite team sport, at the Jaipur Grounds in Delhi. Playing for the 'Taj' side against the 'Qtab', the Prince scored two goals – to the delight of the locals.

Prince Charles finished his Nepalese tour with a three-day trek in the foothills of the Himalayas, accompanied by Prince Dhirendra, the brother of the King of Nepal. Their native guide was the experienced mountaineer, Pertemba Sherpa, who had twice scaled Mount Everest, the first time with the 1975 British expedition led by Chris Bonington.

The trek was through the beautiful Pokhara Valley in the heart of Nepal, dominated by the giant Annapurna Range and by the Machapuchare Himal or 'Fishtail Mountain', which formed a spectacular backdrop for the picture on this page of Prince Charles at the start of his walk.

The Queen in the South Pacific, October 1982

In honoured chief tradition, the Queen is rowed ashore in a dug-out canoe as her welcome to Tuvalu, the former Ellice Islands. The Duke of Edinburgh was similarly perched in state in a following canoe, and they were both thus carried in procession up the beach. I had undertaken the long trip across the world almost entirely with this picture in mind and it proved worth the effort. It was not difficult to photograph, for the canoe moved slowly, but everything depended on the weather. If there had been rain that day, a launch would have brought the Queen ashore from *Britannia*, which served as a floating home for return hospitality during the tour, as well as an ideal means of reaching the widely scattered island countries of the South Pacific.

The small group of pressmen had arrived in Tuvalu in less style and more conventionally, in a specially chartered light aircraft that could land on the island's tiny airstrip. A remote Pacific island four hundred miles north had formed our stop-over. Here, as petrol barrels were rolled out for refuelling the plane, we were served our 'in flight' refreshment. We watched with some amusement as coconuts were cut from a nearby tree, split open with a deft swing of a machete and served with a giggle by our native stewardess.

Replying in blazing heat to a speech of welcome to the Solomon Islands *(opposite)*; a reviving cup of tea during the visit to the tiny island republic of Nauru *(above)*; and driving round the Reuben Uatioa Parade Ground in Kiribati, the former Gilbert Islands *(below)*.

As their last engagement in Tuvalu, the Queen – using the shade of an umbrella – and the Duke of Edinburgh – protected by his straw hat – visited the Maritime School.

The friendliness of the people of Tuvalu was remarkable. With some time on our hands after the Queen had left on *Britannia* to sail to Fiji, we strolled around the island and were invited by a kindly old villager to sit and share a coconut in the shade of the meeting house. We learned about the way of life there and, to our astonishment, that we were in fact chatting with an ex-Prime Minister of the country who had flown to England as a guest at the Royal Wedding.

The Queen in California, February–March 1983

Gales, storms and floods in increasing strength followed the Queen from the day of her arrival on the royal yacht *Britannia* in San Diego *(above)*, where she toured ships of the US Pacific Fleet anchored in the harbour. A week later the itinerary – returning to *Britannia* to sleep each night and sailing up the coast on her – had to be abandoned because of the impossible weather conditions and the Queen and the Duke of Edinburgh flew rather than sailed into Santa Barbara to meet President and Mrs Reagan. The welcoming ceremony was hastily rearranged to take place within the shelter of the aircraft hangar *(right)*.

It was a tribute to America's organizational abilities – down to the white tape marking the standing positions for the official party – that there were no hitches. It may look as if I took this picture on my own but there were as many as a hundred and fifty reporters and photographers on the specially erected tiered stand only thirty feet away from the Queen and the President.

The Prince and Princess of Wales in Australia and New Zealand, March–April 1983

This was the first overseas tour for Princess Diana, and the first too for a royal baby. The accent was very much on youth and many of the vast crowds that turned out to welcome the Prince and Princess were schoolchildren. In Bunbury, south of Perth, the couple drove in an open-top Land Rover to give the enthusiastic children gathered there a better view. They were even more enthusiastic when Prince Charles announced that they would be getting an extra day's holiday at his request.

   This shot was taken from the special camera-truck being driven in front of the Land Rover. Although it is designed on three levels, there is always a rush to get on first to take up the prime position – in the middle of the lowest level. The sight of photographers sprinting for the truck with cameras bashing round their necks usually provides a laugh for the crowds.

Overleaf The day after their arrival in Australia, the Prince and Princess were taken to the outback to visit Ayers Rock, the spectacular red sandstone monolith which for centuries has been sacred to the Aborigines. It made a dramatic background to the photograph of Charles and Diana returning from their walk up the rock.

The visit to the recreated goldrush town, Sovereign Hill, near Ballarat, was one of the jolliest in the tour, which is one reason why I like the picture opposite of a relaxed Princess Diana riding inside the old Ballarat-to-Geelong stagecoach – the Prince rode the shotgun seat on the top.

A different kind of occasion was the Government House garden party in Auckland, New Zealand, hosted by the royal couple. It was held on ANZAC Day, following a remembrance service attended by a tiny remnant of survivors from Gallipoli. I must have seemed a strange sight standing on a chair – borrowed from a clarinet player in the band – in the middle of the neatly clipped Government House lawn to get the above picture of the Princess over the heads of the guests. I wanted to catch the Princess's undoubted talent for showing a genuine and appropriate interest in the people she meets.

Overleaf Prince Charles flying an Australian Air Force Hawker Siddeley 748, the same type of plane as used by the Queen's Flight, from Bendigo en route to Woomargama in New South Wales, where he and the Princess were to rejoin Prince William. The Prince of Wales is an experienced pilot and likes to fly himself whenever the opportunity arises, but to get a good photograph of him at the controls is not easy. Even if you are close enough to the aircraft, light tends to reflect from the cockpit window. On this occasion, the soft glow of the evening sun was ideal.

A sleepy Prince William (*opposite*) is carried off the plane by his nanny, Barbara Barnes, on his arrival in New Zealand. His parents had already disembarked and all cameras were glued to the door of the plane waiting for the world's youngest superstar to appear.

The Prince was driven off from the airport to Government House, Auckland, where he remained during his parents' two-week tour, and it was on the lawns there that a photocall was arranged. Some forty photographers were present – an indication of what is in store for Prince William – and the nine-month-old baby delighted everybody, not least his parents, by demonstrating his newly acquired skill of standing up, with a little support from his dad.

There was concern during the New Zealand tour over threatened Maori protests against what they felt was the loss of their tribal homelands in the 1840 Treaty of Waitangi. Prince Charles helped calm feelings by his peace-making public speeches, and he and the Princess won many over in their personal appearances. The 'hongi', the traditional Maori nose-rubbing welcome, was a new experience for the Princess (*above*, at Gisborne); it's also not an easy thing to photograph. A little too soon or too late and you miss the point of the picture.

The tour ended memorably, as the Prince and Princess were paddled to Waitangi by eighty Maori warriors lining each side of an intricately carved war canoe. Large numbers of Maoris had gathered to welcome them at the spot where the peace treaty between Queen Victoria and the Maoris had been signed.

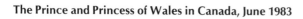

The Prince and Princess of Wales in Canada, June 1983

The staccato whirr of more than thirty Nikon motor-drives – fondly known as the Nikon choir – greeted the Prince and Princess of Wales as they arrived in period costume for a barbecue at historic Fort Edmonton. Prince Charles's suit was a model of that worn by Edward VII when, as Prince of Wales, he had visited Canada, and Princess Diana's pink and cream silk dress, with its lace underskirt, bustle and short train, was a recreation of an 1878 fashionable day dress.

A contrast in style: the Queen in the mother-of-pearl necklace and head-dress of stephanotis flowers presented to her at a South Sea Island feast in Tuvalu *(above left)*; and in more traditional jewels for a state banquet in Fiji *(above right)*.

The Queen in Italy, October 1980

Opposite: The Queen returning from an historic meeting at the Vatican, when the titular head of the Church of England paid her respects to Pope John Paul II. The important picture expected from this visit, of the Queen and the Pope together, was spoilt by the positioning of the microphones, which partially blocked their faces from the only camera position available.

Overleaf The Queen and the Duke of Edinburgh with President Pertini inspecting the Guard of Honour at Quirinale Palace in Rome.

The Queen at Treetops, Kenya, in November 1983, escorted by Mr R.J.Prickett, the 'White Hunter' guide to this famous wildlife area. As a young woman, the Queen – then Princess Elizabeth – had stayed here overnight, lodged in the high wooden platform overlooking waterhole and jungle, on her tour of East Africa with Prince Philip in 1952. It was on her return from Treetops to the nearby Royal Lodge, Sagana, that news of King George VI's death reached her.

Princess Elizabeth is known to have been captivated by her stay at Treetops, then a much more primitive building hidden in the thick of the forest. It is a fascinating place and one of my own most enjoyable experiences on this trip was to have spent the night there and seen elephants and rhinos come to drink at the waterhole just thirty feet below my balcony. It gave a boost to my long-term ambition to see and photograph the more remote reserves in Africa.

Together with my colleagues, I was guilty on this occasion of putting the Queen at risk in the interests of a more memorable picture. For the Queen and Treetops to be in the same frame – and that after all was the only way to illustrate the historical visit – we used our powers of persuasion to get agreement for the Queen to cross to the far side of the waterhole. This in fact meant her standing relatively unprotected in wild animal territory, watched at no great distance by one of Africa's most unpredictable animals – the buffalo.

A few months after the Queen's visit, I learnt from Mr Prickett that the buffalo watching the strange antics at his waterhole on that day had sadly had to be shot when he had charged one of the Treetops staff.

THE ROMANCE

Rumours of an engagement between Prince Charles and Lady Diana Spencer had been mounting steadily since the autumn of 1980 and the announcement was finally made from Buckingham Palace on 24 February 1981. The demand for good pictures of the happy couple was huge and worldwide; after years of photographing the bachelor Prince Charles, this was an important time for me. Knowing that if I did not get the picture right on the day of the engagement there would not be another chance was both an incentive and a cause for nerves. That the Princess is a photographer's delight, and clearly also Prince Charles's, makes the pictures of the couple here among my favourites.

The more formal photograph of the wedding itself is important to me in a different way, not least for its preparation. The position I had for the wedding was over the West door. This meant I would only see the faces of Prince Charles and his bride as they walked back down the aisle after the marriage. In those few moments I wanted to shoot a long lens close-up of the couple on a 300 mm, a more general scene on an 85 mm and a wide-angle shot to show the whole wedding setting. The 300 mm would have to be focused continually as they walked down the aisle but it would be possible to pre-focus both the 85 mm and the wide-angle lens. I planned to clamp and electronically connect three motor-driven Nikons together so that whenever I fired the camera with the 300 mm lens the other two cameras would be taking their pictures at the same time. I went to the trouble and expense of having a firm of specialist camera engineers make a bracket to clamp all the cameras together on one large tripod. What wonderful planning – I thought! The day I collected the custom-built bracket my pass arrived for the wedding, with very firm instructions that no motor-driven cameras were to be used at the wedding ceremony. Despite this set-back I was able – by using clamps and tripods and firing cameras with both hands – to get the three different shots that I wanted. The big general view is my favourite.

The Prince and Princess posed for photographers on the viewing deck of *Britannia* before setting off on their honeymoon cruise – destination most definitely a secret from the world's press. The naval press officer had arranged for two photographic positions, either on the quay itself just below the ship or on the roof of a nearby building. I chose the roof position, looking down on the couple, which gave me the picture opposite and also one of the Prince and Princess holding hands that won for me the Martini Award for the best royal photograph of 1981.

When the long-awaited engagement announcement was made in February 1981, I was out of the office and the message to go to Buckingham Palace for the official engagement photocall finally reached me with only minutes to spare. I was casually dressed and, with no time to go home to change, I dashed to buy a tie from the nearest shop and rushed to the Palace. The couple were standing on the terrace only about ten feet away and Lady Diana, not yet used to the noise of motor-driven cameras, teased that I was just showing off with mine. This picture turned out to be a favourite with the royal couple, who ordered copies of it for their personal use, and it was also selected for the Royal Engagement Commemorative postage stamp in twenty-two Commonwealth countries.

Opposite I had a dramatic view of the Royal Wedding from my position high up over the West door of St Paul's Cathedral and this picture was taken as the Prince and Princess made their way down the aisle after the service on 29 July 1981.

This romantic setting by the bank of the River Dee was chosen for the photocall on 19 August, just after Prince Charles and Princess Diana had returned from their honeymoon cruise to spend the remainder of their holiday at Balmoral. The tanned Prince and Princess were obviously dotty about each other and the resulting intimate pictures give no hint that this peaceful beauty spot was being shared at the time with forty cameramen.

News of the photocall at Balmoral in August 1981, when these pictures were taken, had come in time for me to travel from London to Aberdeen by air. But not so earlier in the year when I had learnt at 10 o'clock one night of a photocall set for early the next morning at Balmoral. Too late for a flight, I set off with my wife Eileen as co-driver to drive through the night, fortified by a flask of coffee, some biscuits and a sense of the ridiculous. We did the thousand-mile round trip from London for a photocall that lasted less than five minutes!

The Prince and Princess on a skiing holiday near Vaduz in Liechtenstein posed for photographers at the start of their visit *(opposite)*. Another thousand miles for another three-minute photocall but it was worth it. The unexpected intimate picture above was taken when the couple were at a sports display in Newcastle, Australia, and that below when they were in Edmonton during the Canada tour.

BY INVITATION

Photographing the Royal Family is my job but to be one of a small corps of photographers following their activities is very different to being personally commissioned to take official portraits. When in January 1982 I was invited by the Queen's Press Secretary, Michael Shea, to take the official eighteenth birthday pictures of Prince Edward, I was of course very pleased to be chosen but was also very nervous. I had never before worked so closely with a member of the Royal Family, and I knew that whatever photographs I took would come in for close scrutiny by picture editors and photographers I had worked with for years.

My style is informal and not therefore in the usual tradition of official royal portraits. I wanted to keep a natural feel to the pictures and, knowing that Prince Edward had a labrador, Frances, I thought that the dog would be a useful prop in making the session more informal. I asked for her to be brought down from Sandringham to London for the photo session – a request which may have raised a few eyebrows at Sandringham – and, apart from playing an important role in the pictures, I think that she did indeed help calm nerves on both sides. I was delighted with the coverage that the pictures were given in hundreds of newspapers and magazines in this country and overseas, and knew that the pictures had been a real success when one of them was chosen for the cover of *Dog World*!

Just before Christmas of that same year, I had another call, this time from Victor Chapman, Press Secretary to the Prince and Princess of Wales, passing on an invitation from the royal couple to photograph them with Prince William at home in Kensington Palace. The couple were to visit Australia and New Zealand in the spring and official portraits were wanted to mark the forthcoming very important tour. I was delighted to accept the invitation but I had plenty of time for nerves afterwards – the whole of Christmas and January, for the session was booked for 1 February.

When the day arrived, I had had little sleep the night before – not finally from nerves but from my new responsibilities as a doting dad. My wife Eileen had just returned from hospital with our baby daughter Lucy, born just a week earlier. It was a very short history of parenthood to share with Prince Charles and Princess Diana but it made a good talking point that day. During the session there were only three of us present, plus of course Prince William for his pictures, because I had deliberately chosen to work as I do normally, without assistants.

Afterwards Princess Diana invited me back to the Palace to show her the pictures personally. Prince William, sitting on his mother's knee, joined in the meeting, gurgling appreciatively at his own portraits and earning for himself a laughing rebuke from his mother for being so vain.

Prince William was just over seven months old at this time, with two front teeth to his credit. He remained in happy mood throughout the session, making an excellent photographer's model in his white and blue silk romper suit. He was not yet crawling but he could raise himself up, and his delightful expression in this picture was due to the antics of his mother, who was attracting his attention towards my camera.

The photographs here and overleaf were taken in the Princess of Wales' sitting-room at Kensington Palace. I wanted to make the scene as relaxed as possible so there was no special placing of furniture or tidying away of the usual objects in the room. Prince William cuddled his toy koala bear – not a random choice, for these photographs were taken to mark the forthcoming tour of Australia and New Zealand.

The clothes worn by Prince Charles and Princess Diana were their personal choice, though I had put in a request for Prince Charles not to wear anything too dark. His choice of an open-necked shirt and yellow jumper I much appreciated. Apart from being a form of dress he is not usually seen in, it helped the relaxed, informal tone of the pictures.

For a deliberate contrast of style, the Prince and Princess later in the session changed into less casual clothes and posed for a formal portrait in the elegant setting of the drawing-room at Kensington Palace.

I would like to think that this wonderful smile was specially due to me but in fact behind me was Prince Charles providing the real inspiration for it.

These official portraits of Prince Edward were issued to celebrate his eighteenth birthday on 10 March 1982. It was a bitterly cold January day when they were taken but I wanted to photograph the Prince out of doors, relaxed and casual. As it turned out, I was lucky with the choice of day for it had snowed the day before and did so again the day after. If Prince Edward felt cold as he posed patiently in the grounds of Buckingham Palace, he made no complaint about it.

I think that it helped that his black labrador, Frances, joined him for the shot below by the lake in Buckingham Palace garden; animals – provided that they don't steal the show – can make fine props. The Prince's dog behaved very well, apart perhaps from showing rather more interest in the ducks on the lake than the photographic session. The aim was for an informal look to the pictures and so preoccupied was I with the job in hand that asking the Prince to sit on a pile of cold, damp leaves seemed a perfectly reasonable request. Fortunately the picture proved a popular one. The day of its release for publication happened to be Budget Day as well as Prince Edward's birthday, which gave rise to press congratulations to the Prince mixed with a few to the royal household for setting a good example of economy by turning down Prince Edward's trouser hems!

OFF DUTY

Some of the most unusual and delightful pictures of the Royal Family come from their off duty moments. It is accepted by members of the Royal Family that when they attend public events, such as a day at the races, a polo match, the Badminton Horse Trials, Cowes Week and other sporting and horse events – whether as competitors or spectators – photographers will be present.

During the polo season, Prince Charles may play up to five matches a week, mostly at Windsor. Princess Diana and other members of the family quite often turn up to watch him and it is at such times that you are likely to get good informal photographs. To cover every match would be impossible, so I try to guess which are likely to provide the best pictures.

One event that often produces good pictures is the carriage driving competition at the Windsor Horse Show each May. The Duke of Edinburgh takes part and the Queen and other members of the Royal Family turn out to watch him. Dressed in casual clothes, they often go unrecognized as they mingle with the crowd of spectators. The course covers a wide area so the organizers provide photographers with a Land Rover to get from one stage of the event to the next. Arriving at one of the obstacles with only seconds to spare before the Duke's carriage was due, our driver, in his haste, failed to recognize the lady in tweed skirt and brogues and deposited us only inches from the Queen and Prince Edward. As the Land Rover door was thrown open it was caught by Prince Edward and we rather sheepishly clambered out. It might seem surprising but until our arrival no one in the crowd had realized that they had been standing almost shoulder to shoulder with their monarch!

In Scotland to cover the Royal Family at the Braemar Games, I was delighted to spot from the road Prince Charles returning from a morning's salmon fishing on the River Dee with his labrador, Harvey, in September 1980.

Princess Diana, in a red
maternity coat, chats in
the paddock at the
Cheltenham Races, March
1982. Although reputedly
wary of horses since a
riding fall in childhood, she
enjoys joining other
members of the Royal
Family at the regular racing
and polo occasions.

As the proud owner of a fine racing stable and a lover of horses for their own sake, the Queen Mother is a familiar figure at race meetings around the country – here at Cheltenham in 1982. She is always a favourite with photographers because she has a knack of looking towards the camera so that everyone gets a picture, and her famous smile has produced many a lovely picture.

The Queen, a keen amateur photographer, is here using her Leica camera to photograph Prince Philip competing at the 1982 Royal Windsor Horse Show. It is not just when she is off duty that the Queen can be seen with a camera. On overseas tours she often uses a small gold Rollei camera which can be slipped easily into her bag.

My own photograph of Prince Philip competing at Windsor was taken during the International Driving Grand Prix of 1980. The event includes a tricky obstacle course and for a good picture of this you need to pick out two or three obstacles to cover and hope that one will produce the picture you want. In this case I used an 85 mm lens to record Prince Philip tackling the sandpit with the Queen's team of bays.

Prince Charles taking part in the 1978 Quorn Cross-Country Team Event, a new sport in which he had just become interested. It involves tough racing in teams of four, with formidable natural fences en route; he is said to have joked off his falls as 'good practice for parachuting'.

A pensive Prince Andrew looks on as his fellow-competitors, who included Mark Phillips and ex-King Constantine of Greece, take part in a clay-pigeon shoot near Chester, August 1980, an event organized for charity and which the Prince's shooting skills helped his team to win.

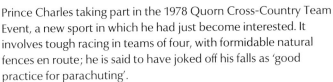

Opposite Princess Anne at the three-day European Equestrian Championships in Kiev, Russia, in 1973. Back-lighting always creates an attractive soft effect and here the Princess had stopped for just a moment, back-lit against the trees. This was one of only two frames taken before she moved on again.

Overleaf After an afternoon at Ascot Races, Prince Charles usually plays polo at Smith's Lawn, Windsor, and he is seen here before the match with his constant shadow – the bodyguard who has been with him for over twelve years and who joins the Prince when skiing, windsurfing or swimming but has managed to avoid risking his neck on a polo pony.

Binoculars are often used by the Royal Family at horse events. For the Queen, at the 1980 Badminton Horse Trials *(above)* and for Princess Michael of Kent, at the 1982 Windsor Horse Show *(opposite)*, mini-binocolars are the order of the day. Prince Charles takes a more powerful pair to watch his competitors at the Fernie Hunt Cross-Country Team Event in 1979 *(below)*.

Previous pages
After attending the Sandringham flower show in July 1982, the Queen Mother with her corgi and a friend took a bracing walk along a quiet beach in Norfolk.

Prince Charles, still tanned from his recent Canadian tour, carries the fourteen-month-old Prince William from the plane that the Prince of Wales had himself just piloted to Aberdeen. They and Princess Diana, who had come down the steps ahead, were en route to their annual holiday at Balmoral in August 1983.

A jolly Prince William shows off his walking skills at a photocall in the garden of his home at Kensington Palace in December 1983. He was eighteen months old and seemed amused by the bank of assembled cameramen. After giving us the 'once over' he decided that he had done his duty and he had to be retrieved by Prince Charles as he headed off for the garden gate.

This power-boat was a present to Prince Charles from the wife of President Marcos of the Philippines and is named *Imelda* after her. It is kept in the Scilly Isles, where Prince Charles has a small holiday bungalow, Tamarisk, which forms part of his inheritance as Duke of Cornwall. Here, he was out for a spin during a visit to his Duchy estates in April 1982.

The Queen is usually to be seen being chauffered in style but off duty at Windsor she often drives herself on the private roads of the park. Her passenger in the back as she was leaving a polo match at Smith's Lawn in May 1977 was Colonel Sir John Miller, the crown equerry and as such responsible for cars as well as horses and carriages – not that the Queen's immaculately maintained 1960s Vauxhall seems likely to break down.

For several years running, Prince Charles joined his close friends, Charles and Patti Palmer-Tomkinson, for a skiing holiday in the beautiful Swiss village of Klosters. In early 1981 when the photograph opposite was taken, the announcement of his engagement was imminent and there was a lot of press interest in his trip. The year before he had succeeded in getting some of his own back on the press with a splendid leg-pull. We listened with some concern when Patti Palmer-Tomkinson appeared from the chalet to announce that Prince Charles would not be able to ski that day because of a slight fall on the stairs, and her Uncle Harry would be joining them instead. A figure appeared from the chalet muttering about the younger generation having no stamina and it took a few moments for the startled cameramen to realize who was behind the large false nose, moustache and glasses.

In January 1984 Prince Charles and Princess Diana went on their
second skiing holiday to Vaduz. This picture was taken at a
photocall on their first day out on the slopes, in the company of
the Prince and Princess of Liechtenstein. Although Princess Diana
is no novice on skis, Prince Charles has by far the greater
experience and skill, even if the Swiss are reported to have
compared his skiing, rather unkindly, to a farmer's – more
courage than style.

For anyone interested in horse-racing, the Derby is almost a compulsory event and the Royal Family is usually there in force. Princess Anne and the Duke of Edinburgh are seen here in the paddock between races in June 1983.

Smiles of celebration: the Queen was watching Prince Charles's team win a polo match at Smith's Lawn, Windsor, in June 1980 – she afterwards presented one of the prizes to her son; the Duke of Edinburgh had just been competing successfully in one of the stages of the carriage driving event at Windsor Great Park in September 1982.

Opposite The Queen Mother, with the Duke of Edinburgh in the background, at the 1983 Derby. She and the Queen are both enthusiastic race-horse owners and the Queen Mother has over three hundred wins to her credit, though never the Derby itself. The sticks are her first love but she is clearly in her element on all race-days.

Prince Edward windsurfing off Cowes in August 1980. He and
Prince Charles had joined their father on the royal yacht *Britannia*
for Cowes Regatta week, which the Duke of Edinburgh regularly
attends. The Queen does not accompany him but the Duke is
joined by other members of the family. On this occasion Prince
Edward had taken advantage of the early morning quiet to go out
and enjoy a favourite sport.

Prince Charles out for a peaceful ride during the Badminton Horse Trials in 1979 *(opposite)*. He was there not as a competitor but as a spectator, watching both his sister and her husband take part. The above display of Princess Anne's horsemanship was at the Tidworth Horse Trials in 1974.

Overleaf Surrounded by polo tackle, Prince Charles gets ready to play a match at Smith's Lawn, Windsor, in 1975.

COVER GIRL PRINCESS

In the years I spent photographing the bachelor Prince Charles it was obvious that when he chose his bride there would be intense interest from the general public and the world's press. None of us, however, could have anticipated the phenomenal interest that would be created by the nineteen-year-old Lady Diana Spencer, who in just a few years has become the world's number one cover girl. Every major magazine, whether news or fashion, has featured her on the cover – in some cases many times.

Young and pretty, with her fair hair, blue eyes and beautiful complexion, the Princess of Wales is most people's image of the ideal princess, and with such looks it is hard to go wrong photographing her. Added to that she has an obvious charm, a natural response to people, particularly children, that creates an atmosphere of warmth and friendliness wherever she goes – and gives plenty of opportunities for delightful pictures. If I sound like a devoted fan, I have to say that even the most blasé of journalists and photographers have all at some stage been captivated by the Princess, particularly if they have had the opportunity for a few words with her.

On her tours and public appearances at home she has appeared in a series of stunning outfits, mostly the work of young British designers and often matched with equally stylish hats by John Boyd. Her evening outfits especially have drawn everyone's attention, and the remarkable interest means that the rush to photograph her is greater than ever when she is due to appear for an evening engagement. The Princess, however, has a problem in being the centre of all eyes: if she wears too many new outfits, journalists comment on her extravagant wardrobe; if she wears the same outfit too often, there is disappointment, particularly among her photographers. Men are often criticised for not taking a lot of interest in what their wives or girlfriends wear but when it comes to the regulars who photograph Princess Diana, the chatter about fashion details that goes on between us is worthy of the most ardent women fashion critics.

On a walkabout in Brisbane during the tour of Australia and New Zealand in April 1983. The Princess's clothes were an eye-catching feature of this visit and of her later tour of Canada, and here she was wearing a blue and white silk dress designed by Donald Campbell and a white tricorn-shaped hat by her favourite milliner, John Boyd.

Princess Diana wore this stunning ballgown, designed by Bellville Sassoon, for the opening of the Splendours of the Gonzaga exhibition at the Victoria and Albert Museum on 4 November 1981. She looked every inch the fairy-tale princess and it could not have been a better timed photograph, for the next day came the announcement that the Princess was expecting her first child.

Arriving at the Barbican Arts Centre for a charity gala performance in March 1982. The red taffeta dress is another Bellville Sassoon design, which the Princess wore with a diamond necklace – part of the Royal Family heirlooms referred to by the Queen as 'granny's chips'. These were not details I took in at the time, for my view was blocked at the last minute by a row of burly policemen and, with no time for discussion, I quickly crouched to the ground to shoot this picture through their legs.

Princess Diana at the foot
of the ski slopes at Vaduz,
Liechtenstein. This was
taken at a photocall on the
first day of her skiing
holiday with Prince Charles
in January 1984.

Watching Prince Charles play polo at Cirencester, near their Highgrove home, in the summer of 1983. The blouse, by Jan Velvelden, had been part of a formal outfit that the Princess had worn on the New Zealand tour; worn casually, it looked stunning.

In Charlottetown, Canada, on the tour in June 1983. The Princess has a fondness for small veiled hats, which can be a problem when photographing because of the shadows created by the veil. But if the light is right, the result is particularly flattering.

This summery red and white straw hat saw use on both the Australian and Canadian tours. Here, the Princess was wearing it at Altona, Australia.

In Charlo, Canada, in June 1983 when the Princess met Indians of the Mic Mac tribe, one of the largest Indian tribes in New Brunswick province. She wore the same off-white straw hat and navy and white suit as on her visit to Auckland earlier that year.

For the inauguration of the new police headquarters in Ottawa, Princess Diana chose the outfit designed by Jasper Conran which she had originally worn for the Trooping the Colour ceremony in 1982. Harsh sunlight can be very unflattering because of the strong shadows it creates but it worked to advantage here, reflecting off the paving stones to lighten the shadow under the Princess's wide-brimmed hat.

This picture was taken in Canberra as the Princess posed with Prince Charles and the Australian Prime Minister, Robert Hawke, and his wife, at the start of the Prince and Princess of Wales' visit in March 1983.

Princess Diana was here attending a Variety Club luncheon at the Guildhall, London, in July 1983. She paused briefly on the step and I shot this picture with a 600 mm lens.

Some of the widely varied styles that have helped make Princess Diana a leader of fashion throughout the world and a continuing pleasure to photograph. Her distinctive hats are a feature on many occasions but at other times she may go bare-headed or, on formal evenings, wear the traditional jewelled tiaras of royalty. At a reception in Tasmania, the Princess wore the Spencer tiara, which she had worn at her wedding, *(above)*; and the diamond and pearl drop tiara, a present from the Queen, was the crowning touch for a Government House dinner in Canberra *(above centre)*.

OFF GUARD

The public face of royalty rarely slips but there are always the unexpected moments – when arrangements don't go quite according to plan, animals make up their own minds, the weather takes a turn for the worst – and a very human face is shown to the world. Even the Queen, well known for remaining composed in practically any situation, produced an expressive grimace when tramping through the wet at the Windsor Horse Show and getting soaked at the Trooping the Colour ceremony. I too got drenched on the other side of the camera, despite some protection from my large waterproof cape, but at least no one would think of taking my picture.

I always carry wet weather gear and cloths to wipe the camera lenses in case it rains but as well as being prepared you need luck to catch the off guard moments of the Royal Family. Nobody could have predicted, and clearly not Princess Anne, that her dog would have to be carried down the aircraft steps at Heathrow; I had gone along expecting a fairly routine shot of the Princess returning from holiday. Nor had I expected anything nearly as dramatic from the Badminton Horse Trials in 1982, when Princess Anne was competing. Water jumps always produce a good picture and occasionally a spectacular one if the rider comes off, as Princess Anne unfortunately did here. It was one of those occasions, like Prince Charles capsizing while windsurfing or Princess Diana at the mercy of a fly-away collar, when a motor-driven camera comes into its own. The story is made of frames divided by split seconds, a speed not possible with a manually wound camera.

But it is not just members of the Royal Family who may be caught off guard. I have fond memories of India and a picture that always makes me smile is the one of Prince Charles looking in imminent danger of treading the red carpet of welcome before the frantic carpet-layers could get it all down. Following the path of royalty definitely has its funny moments.

The Queen picking her way through mud to present prizes in driving rain at the Royal Windsor Horse Show in May 1978.

Below Concerned onlookers as the sugar lumps get shared with the polo groom's terrier after the game.

Below, right An eager polo pony taking a nip from the hand that feeds him ...

and *(bottom)* an enthusiastic nuzzle for his master from Harvey the labrador.

Top, opposite and above A breeze outside the Legislature Building in Edmonton, Alberta, and the Princess struggles with an irrepressible grin as her collar takes on a life of its own.

Below Prince Charles in no rush to sample the joys of babies on his New Zealand tour in 1981.

A royal talking-to for one
of the Queen's carriage
horses at the Windsor
Horse Show, May 1980.

The RAF to the rescue as
Princess Anne's dog
refuses the aircraft steps at
Heathrow on returning
from Balmoral in 1981.

A speechless Duke of Edinburgh at the Badminton Horse
Trials in April 1982 *(below)*, and *(opposite)* the Duke unaware
of being upstaged by a Swiss in ancient costume at Rutli,
Switzerland, in April 1980.

Perhaps not as avid a horse-racing fan as some of his relatives, the Duke of Gloucester with his wife at the Derby, June 1981.

Opposite The Queen getting drenched in the final moments of Trooping the Colour in June 1982. The large cape covering my head, the camera and its 600 mm lens enabled me to take this picture.

Prince Charles losing the battle for balance while
windsurfing at Cowes in 1980 . . .

Princess Anne taking a fall at the water jump in the
Badminton Horse Trials of 1982 . . .

. . . and resurfacing unharmed.

Overleaf After-the-last-minute preparations as Prince Charles arrives by plane on his tour of India in December 1980.